DID YOU KNOW?
Kangaroos

DID YOU KNOW?
Kangaroos

young
reed

Contents

Red Kangaroo.

What is a Kangaroo?

● Kangaroos are **mammals** belonging to the **marsupial** family. Young marsupials start life in their mother's **pouch**.

● Within the marsupial family, kangaroos are included in a 'subfamily' called **macropods**. Macro means 'big' and pod means 'foot', so the name translates as **'bigfoot'**.

● The macropod family also includes smaller animals such as wallabies, but the name **kangaroo** is reserved for some of the bigger species such as **Red Kangaroo**, the **Grey Kangaroos** and the **Tree-Kangaroos**.

● Some of the smaller macropod species also include the word 'kangaroo' in their name, such as the **Musky Rat-Kangaroo** of Queensland.

Goodfellow's Tree-Kangaroo.

Musky Rat-Kangaroo.

Facts and Figures

- The Red Kangaroo is the world's **largest marsupial**, measuring more than **two metres** in length and weighing over **ninety kilograms**.

- A group of kangaroos is called a **mob**. A mob can sometimes contain hundreds of animals.

- Male kangaroos are famous for **boxing** and kicking each other as they fight for a mate during the breeding season.

Getting around

● A large kangaroo can leap **ten metres** in a single jump and travel at speeds of **fifty kilometres per hour.**

● Kangaroos are the only large mammals that move around by **hopping** in this way.

● Kangaroos **cannot hop backwards.**

● As well as hopping, kangaroos can **walk around** using all four legs and their tail.

Walking kangaroo.

Special adaptations

● A kangaroo's **hind-legs** are built for **power** and **speed**.

● The front paws are totally different, being much smaller and having **claws** to help with **feeding** and **grooming** the fur.

● Its **tail** acts as a **rudder** and helps to give **balance and direction** when hopping at speed.

13

Where do they live?

● Although they are familiar in zoos across the world, wild kangaroos live only in **Australia** and **New Guinea**.

Australia is home to three ground-living kangaroos — **Red Kangaroo, Eastern Grey Kangaroo** and **Western Grey Kangaroo** — while several species of **Tree-Kangaroos** live in Tropical Queensland and New Guinea.

More than **forty million** kangaroos are estimated to live in Australia, although their numbers declined by more than ten million between 2013 and 2024.

Newborn joey feeding in mum's pouch.
(Geoff Shaw/kangaroo.genome.org.au/Wikimedia Commons)

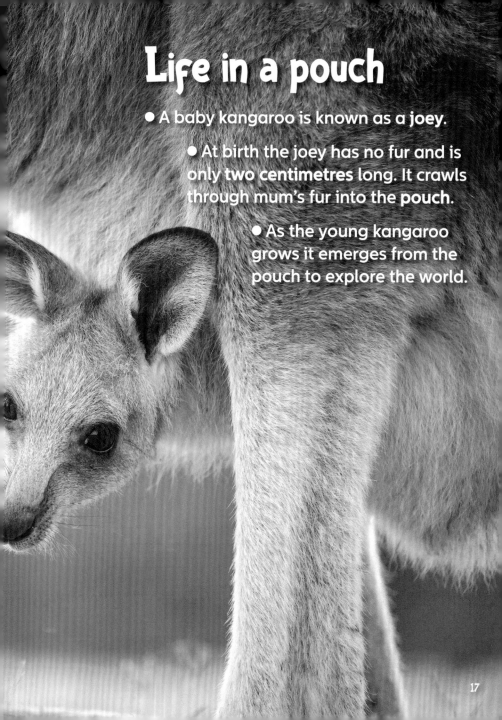

Life in a pouch

- A baby kangaroo is known as a **joey**.

- At birth the joey has no fur and is only **two centimetres** long. It crawls through mum's fur into the **pouch**.

- As the young kangaroo grows it emerges from the pouch to explore the world.

What's for dinner?

- Kangaroos are **herbivores** — they mostly **graze on plants** such as grasses, flowers and leaves.

- They especially like **tender new shoots** of plants.

● Like humans, kangaroo have sharp **incisor** teeth at the front for cutting their food and flat **molars** at the back for grinding it up.

● They are mainly **nocturnal**, meaning that they are active at night.

Taking to the trees

- Tree-Kangaroos are **arboreal**, meaning that they live in trees.

- They can be found in **tropical rainforests**, climbing around in the canopy rather like a kangaroo-shaped possum.

- **Lumholtz's** and **Bennett's Tree-Kangaroos** are found in northern Queensland and there are several other species in New Guinea.

Goodfellow's Tree-Kangaroo from New Guinea.

Lumholtz's Tree-Kangaroo
from Queensland.

Wedge-tailed Eagle.

Dingo.

Threats to Kangaroos

- Humans are the main threat to kangaroos, due to hunting, destruction of their habitat and road-traffic casualties.

Rescued baby kangaroo.

- **Orphaned joeys** are sometimes bottle-fed and raised by humans.

- Kangaroos' **natural** predators include **Dingos** and **Wedge-tailed Eagles.**

First published in 2025 by
New Holland Publishers
Sydney

newhollandpublishers.com

Level 1, 178 Fox Valley Road, Wahroonga, NSW 2076, Australia

A record of this book is held at the National Library of Australia.

ISBN 978 1 92107 386 1

OTHER TITLES IN THE 'DID YOU KNOW?' SERIES:

Meerkat
ISBN 978 1 92107 389 2

Koala
ISBN 978 1 92107 387 8

Lizards
ISBN 978 1 92107 388 5

Penguins
ISBN 978 1 92107 390 8

Red Panda
ISBN 978 1 92107 391 5

For details of these books and hundreds of other Natural History titles see newhollandpublishers.com

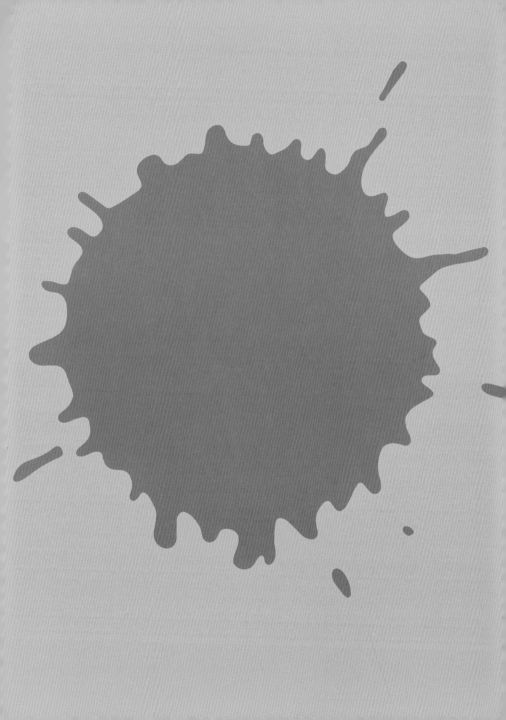